Wedding SHOWERS

From rustic to romantic or colorful, the special themes presented in this book will add excitement to simple wedding showers. Each collection offers invitations and background decorations as well as practical pieces for serving refreshments and fun ideas for creating memorable keepsakes.

LEISURE ARTS, INC.

Rustic Wedding Shower

Project instructions given on pages 3-7.

Invitation

SHOPPING LIST

For each invitation:

- ☐ 5" x 6$\frac{3}{4}$" piece of printed cardstock
- ☐ 4" x 6" piece of burlap
- ☐ white cardstock
- ☐ two 12" lengths of paper twine
- ☐ $\frac{1}{4}$" hole punch
- ☐ computer and printer

To make the Invitation:

1. Use your computer to print the shower information in the desired font on white cardstock, keeping the type within a 3" x 4$\frac{1}{2}$" area. Leaving 1" above the type, trim the cardstock to 3$\frac{1}{2}$" x 5$\frac{1}{2}$".
2. Centering each piece, stack the cardstock and burlap pieces. Punch two holes approximately 1$\frac{1}{2}$" apart at the top of the stack through all layers.
3. Beginning on the front of the invitation, hold the lengths together and insert the twine through one hole and out the other hole; repeat. Trim the twine ends as desired.

Backdrop

Create a striking backdrop for your buffet table with 3"w strips of red- and natural-colored burlap ribbons and 3"w torn strips of assorted fabrics in varying lengths. Tie the strips to a large dowel for hanging.

Create a relaxing, informal setting-indoors or out.

Box Lunch

Provide a simple box lunch for your guests! Pack a barbeque sandwich, fruit cup, and a brownie in a purchased window box. Tie the napkin, straw, and fork to the top of the box with paper twine. Provide bottled drinks in a divided crate with a chalkboard painted sign labeled "Watering Hole" with chalk.

Date Night Jar

Treat the bride and groom to a jar full of date night ideas! Have your guests write their best suggestions on a craft stick and drop them in the bottle.

SHOPPING LIST

- ☐ bottle (ours is approximately 9" tall)
- ☐ 18" length of 1$^{1}/_{2}$"w ribbon
- ☐ jute
- ☐ bakers twine
- ☐ black chalkboard paint
- ☐ paintbrush
- ☐ chalk
- ☐ large craft sticks
- ☐ small metal bucket (ours is approximately 3$^{1}/_{2}$" tall)
- ☐ colored pencils
- ☐ 2" diameter wood tag
- ☐ large wood slice (ours is approximately 11" x 13")

To make the Date Night Jar:

1. Use the chalkboard paint to paint a heart on the bottle and a scalloped oval on the wood slice; allow to dry. Write "Date Jar" on the heart with chalk.
2. Tie the jute and ribbon around the neck of the bottle.
3. Use colored pencils to decorate and write on the tag. Use jute and bakers twine to tie the tag to the bucket handle.
4. Place craft sticks and colored pencils in the bucket.
5. Display the jar and bucket on the wood slice.

Make it a colorful celebration with box lunches, cool beverages and date night ideas.

Flower Pouch

SHOPPING LIST

- ☐ 1/2 yard of burlap fabric
- ☐ 1 1/4 yards of rope
- ☐ 7 1/2" x 6" chalkboard
- ☐ chalk
- ☐ 3/4 yard of red paper twine
- ☐ assorted flowers
- ☐ poster board
- ☐ hand drill and bit
- ☐ clear acrylic spray sealer
- ☐ sewing machine
- ☐ hot glue gun and glue sticks

To make the Pouch:

1. Refer to **Fig. 1** to draw two triangles on the poster board; cut out.

Fig. 1

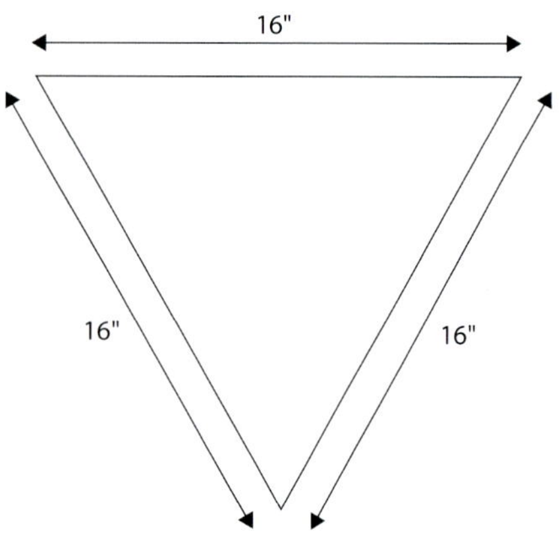

2. Using one of the poster board pieces as a pattern, cut two pieces of burlap 2" larger on all sides than the poster board piece.
3. Sew the burlap triangles together along two sides; turn inside out. Finger press the seams flat. Stitch 1/2" from the sewn sides.
4. Insert the poster board pieces in the burlap pouch.
5. Use scissors to cut a slit through the upper corners of the pouch, through the burlap and the poster board. Insert the rope ends through the holes and knot on the front.
6. Fill the pouch with flowers.
7. Drill holes in top corners of the chalkboard. Use the chalk to draw a monogram on the chalkboard. Spray the chalkboard with spray sealer.
8. Cut the twine in half. Holding the lengths together, insert the jute ends through the holes and knot on the front. Hang the chalkboard over some of the flowers in front. Glue the chalkboard to the pouch front.

Spice things up with simple but oh, so clever ideas.

Potato Chip Bar

Create your own potato chip bar! Place individual servings of either homemade or purchased potato chips in waxed tissue paper-lined cardboard berry containers. Use red cord to tie a chalkboard "Fresh Chips" tag to the container. Use black chalkboard paint and a circle stencil to paint a circle on shaker jars and place assorted seasonings in the jars. Try Ranch, BBQ, Lime, Cheese, Salt & Vinegar, Black Pepper, or Sour Cream and Onion. You can find recipes for these and more on the Internet or simply purchase them. Place it all on a table covered with a black paper table runner and label the seasonings on the paper.

Romantic Wedding Shower

Cookie Tower instructions given on page 14.

Invitation

SHOPPING LIST

For each invitation:

- ☐ 5" x $6\frac{3}{4}$" piece of printed cardstock
- ☐ 4" x 6" piece of green cardstock
- ☐ white cardstock
- ☐ 10" length of $\frac{5}{8}$"w pink satin ribbon
- ☐ $\frac{1}{4}$" hole punch
- ☐ computer and printer

You're invited! Serve up sweetness on a serving tower you can craft in no time.

To make the Invitation:

1. Use your computer to print the shower information in the desired font on white cardstock, keeping the type within a 3" x $4\frac{1}{2}$" area. Leaving 1" above the type, trim the cardstock to $3\frac{1}{2}$" x $5\frac{1}{2}$".
2. Centering each piece, stack the cardstock pieces. Punch two holes approximately $1\frac{1}{2}$" apart at the top of the stack through all layers.
3. Beginning on the front of the invitation, insert the ribbon through one hole and out the other hole; repeat. Trim the ribbon ends as desired.

Tissue Pouf

SHOPPING LIST

For each pouf:

- ☐ ten 20" x 26" sheets of gift wrap tissue paper
- ☐ 2 yards of cotton cord

To make the Pouf:

1. Layer the sheets of tissue paper on top of each other. The sheets can be all one color or a mixture of colors.

2. Beginning on one short end, fold approximately 1" to $1^{1}/_{2}$" pleats across the length of the stack.

3. Fold the stack in half to find the center. Trim the corners of the folded edge diagonally ***(Fig. 1)***. Tie the cord around the center ***(Fig. 2)***.

Fig. 1

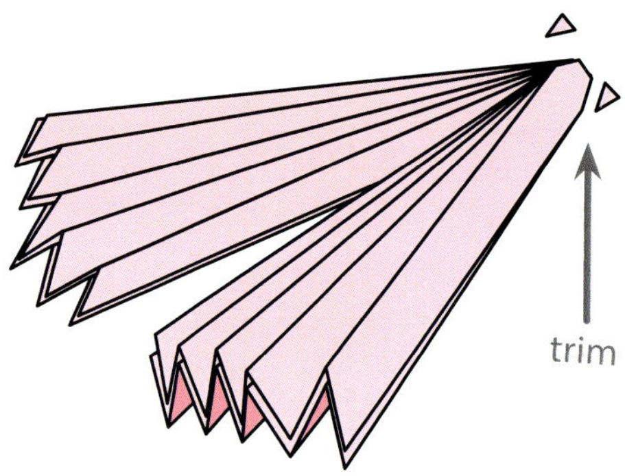

Fig. 2

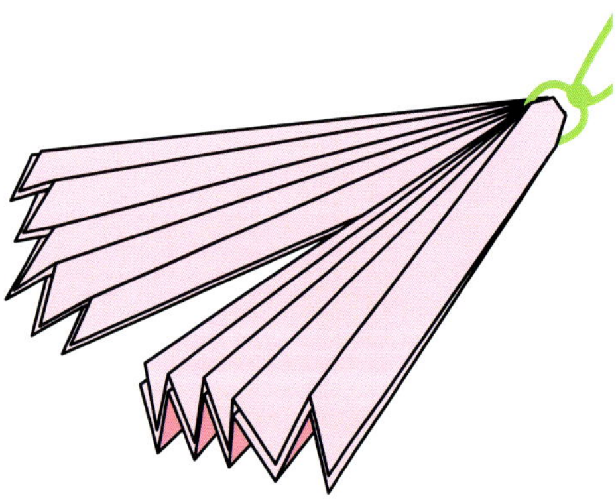

4. Trim the opposite end of the folded tissue paper to a point ***(Fig. 3)***.

Fig. 3

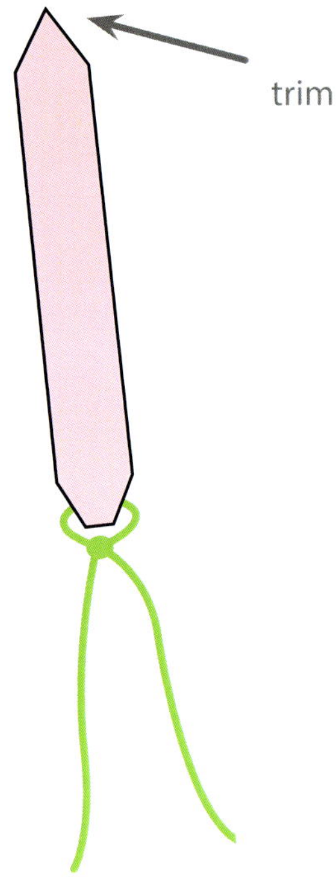

5. Separate the top layer of one side of the folds and pull the layer upward. Continue to separate and pull each layer until you have a nice round pouf.
6. To make smaller poufs, simply trim off more of the folded ends in Step 4.

Just a little paper can create a whole lot of romantic flair.

Bride to Be Banner

SHOPPING LIST

- ☐ ten 4" x 5" pieces of white cardstock
- ☐ metallic gold pigment-based permanent ink pad
- ☐ black and pink acrylic paint
- ☐ 2" alphabet stencils
- ☐ foam spouncer
- ☐ small paintbrush
- ☐ 1/4"w gold metallic trim
- ☐ four 18" lengths of 7/8"w gold metallic ribbon
- ☐ clear tape

To make the Banner:

1. Cut two lengths of trim to tie to the back of the chair.
2. Fold one short edge of each piece of cardstock 1" to the back.
3. Paint a pink heart on one piece of cardstock. Stencil one black letter on each remaining piece of the cardstock.
4. Use the stamp pad to add ink around the edges of each cardstock piece.
5. Place the folded edges of the cardstock over the trim pieces and tape them in place.
6. Tie the banners to the chair. Tie a ribbon length at each end.

Treat Cup

SHOPPING LIST

For each treat cup:

- ☐ paper treat cup with scalloped edge
- ☐ two 6" x 10" pieces of cream tulle
- ☐ $^{3}/_{4}$ yard of $^{1}/_{4}$"w green check ribbon
- ☐ $^{1}/_{4}$" hole punch
- ☐ desired candy

To make the Treat Cup:

1. Punch an even number of holes around the top of the treat cup.
2. Beginning from the outside and leaving tails at the beginning and the end, weave a 18" ribbon length in and out of the holes. Tie the ribbon ends in a bow; trim the ends as desired.
3. Stack the tulle pieces. Place the candy on the tulle. Gather the edges around the candy and knot the remaining length of ribbon around the top. Trim the ribbon and tulle as desired.

Cookie Tower

SHOPPING LIST

- ☐ 12" diameter plastic platter
- ☐ 9" diameter plastic plate
- ☐ 6$^{1}/_{4}$" diameter plastic plate
- ☐ 7$^{1}/_{4}$" diameter plastic bowl
- ☐ two 3$^{1}/_{4}$" diameter plastic cups
- ☐ ivory satin spray paint
- ☐ paper treat cup
- ☐ 2 wood skewers
- ☐ solid pink and floral print scrapbook paper
- ☐ 1 yard of $^{1}/_{4}$"w green check ribbon
- ☐ 2$^{1}/_{4}$" diameter foam craft ball, cut in half
- ☐ $^{5}/_{8}$" alphabet rubber stamps
- ☐ $^{3}/_{8}$" heart rubber stamp
- ☐ black pigment-based permanent ink
- ☐ four 6" x 8" pieces of green tulle
- ☐ decorative-edge scissors
- ☐ 1$^{3}/_{8}$"w heart-shaped paper punch
- ☐ hot glue gun and glue sticks
- ☐ tracing paper
- ☐ rocks to weight the treat cup
- ☐ purchased cookies

To make the Tower:

1. Spray paint the backs ***only*** of the plates and platter. Spray paint the insides ***only*** of the bowl and cups; allow to dry.
2. Glue the bowl, platter, plates, and cups together.
3. Cut a piece of solid pink paper large enough to go around the treat cup and slightly taller than the treat cup. Trim the top edge of the paper with the decorative-edge scissors. Wrap the paper around the treat cup and glue together.
4. Punch a heart from the print scrapbook paper. Glue the heart to the treat cup.
5. Trace the pattern, page 24, onto tracing paper; cut out. Use the pattern to cut four pennants from the print scrapbook paper. Use the stamps and ink to add a message to the pennants.
6. Cut two 9" lengths of ribbon; set aside.
7. Glue the pennants in the center of the remaining length of ribbon.
8. Place a few rocks in the treat cup. Wrap the $^{1}/_{2}$ foam ball with the tulle; place in the cup.
9. Insert the skewers in the foam ball. Tie the remaining ribbon to the skewers. Use the 9" ribbon lengths to tie a bow on each skewer. Place the treat cup on top of the cupcake tower.
10. Place the cookies on the tower.

I ♥ DO

Bride's Advice Book

SHOPPING LIST

- ☐ two 1/4" thick wood boards 6 1/4" x 9"
- ☐ 1" gold alphabet stickers
- ☐ three approximately 1 1/2" diameter fabric flowers
- ☐ assorted silk flowers and leaves
- ☐ 3 mm and 8 mm self-adhesive pearls
- ☐ ivory acrylic paint
- ☐ paintbrush
- ☐ assorted 6" x 8 1/2" pieces of scrapbook paper
- ☐ cotton twine
- ☐ sandpaper
- ☐ hand drill and bit
- ☐ hot glue gun and glue sticks
- ☐ 1/4" hole punch

To make the Book:

1. Drill 3 evenly spaced holes in the same position on each board.
2. Paint the boards with ivory paint; allow to dry. Sand the boards lightly to distress. Be sure to sand along the edges and on the corners.
3. Remove the silk flowers and leaves from their stems. Glue the fabric flowers, silk flowers, and leaves to one board.
4. Adhere the letters to the board.
5. Adhere the pearls to the board.
6. Use the hole punch to punch holes that align with the boards along one edge of the paper pieces.
7. Thread the twine through the holes in the boards and papers; tie twine in a bow and trim the ends.

Colorful Wedding Shower

Project instructions given on pages 20-24.

Invitation

SHOPPING LIST

For each invitation:

- ☐ 5" x $6^{3}/_{4}$" piece of printed cardstock
- ☐ 4" x 6" piece of pink cardstock
- ☐ white cardstock
- ☐ 10" length of $^{5}/_{8}$"w grosgrain ribbon
- ☐ $^{1}/_{4}$" hole punch
- ☐ computer and printer

To make the Invitation:

1. Use your computer to print the shower information in the desired font on white cardstock, keeping the type within a 3" x $4^{1}/_{2}$" area. Leaving 1" above the type, trim the cardstock to $3^{1}/_{2}$" x $5^{1}/_{2}$".
2. Centering each piece, stack the cardstock pieces. Punch two holes approximately $1^{1}/_{2}$" apart at the top of the stack through all layers.
3. Beginning on the front of the invitation, insert the ribbon through one hole and out the other hole; repeat. Trim the ribbon ends as desired.

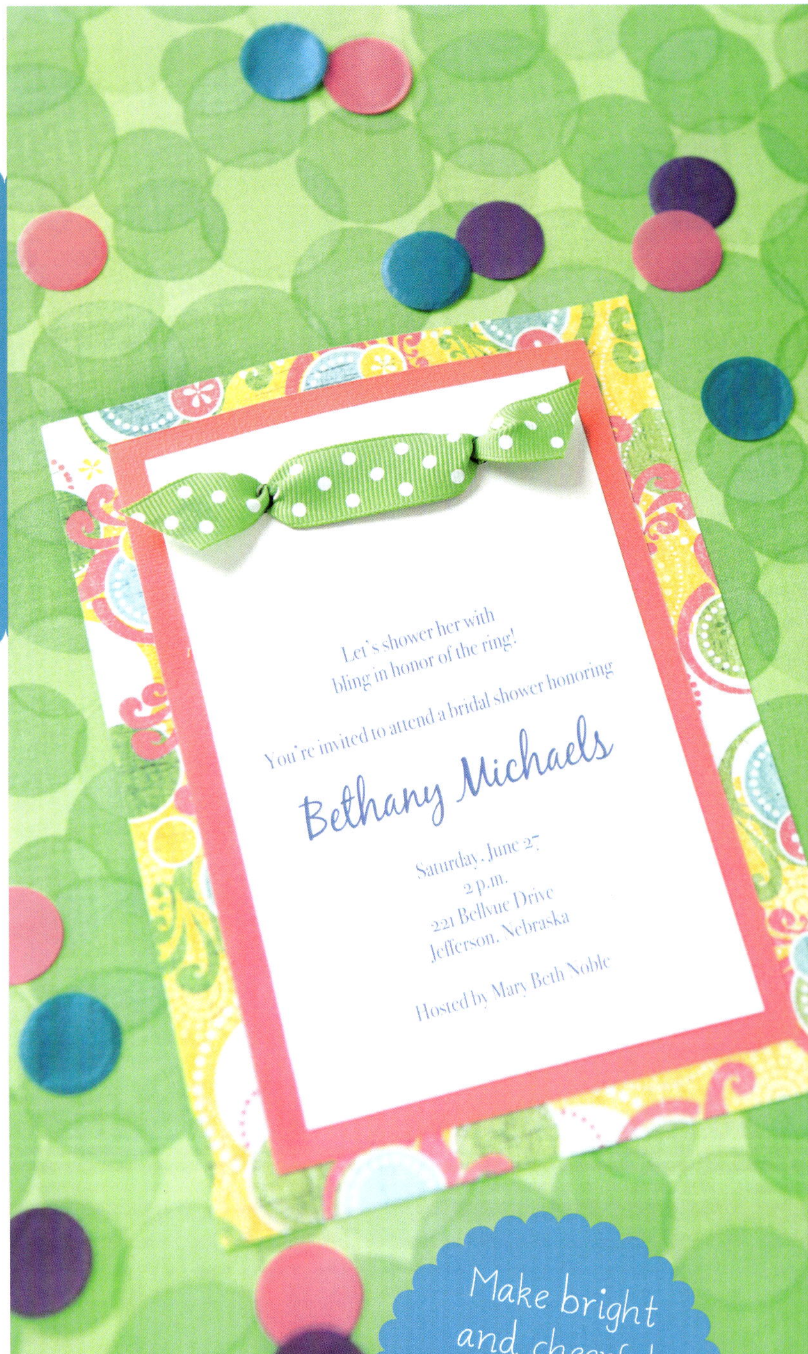

Make bright and cheerful invitations that will not go unnoticed!

Create a keepsake the newlyweds will enjoy reading together on their first anniversary!

Best Wishes Box

Whether at the shower or the reception, invite your guests to write a heart-felt message of love and encouragement to the bride and groom. On their one year anniversary the happy couple can take the messages out and read them one-by-one and remember the outpouring of love from their family and friends.

Our Best Wishes Box is really simple! Just cut a slot in the top of a purchased shadowbox frame. Add paper backgrounds and a photo of the couple. Use alphabet stickers to add their names to the glass on the outside. Cut 3" x 6" pieces of cardstock, fold in half, punch a hole, and tie them closed with satin cord. Add words, such as "Wishes" and "Thoughts" with smaller alphabet stickers. Your guests can write on the cards and drop them in the box!

Paper Flowers

SHOPPING LIST

For each flower:

- ☐ 14" x 27" piece of colored paper for flower
- ☐ 3" diameter circle of colored paper for center
- ☐ cotton string
- ☐ 1/8" hole punch
- ☐ decorative-edge scissors
- ☐ hot glue gun and glue sticks

To make the Flower:

1. Beginning on one short end, fold approximately 1 1/2" pleats across the length of the paper.
2. Fold the paper in half to find the center. Trim the corners of the folded edge diagonally *(Fig. 1)*. Tie an 8" length of string around the center *(Fig. 2)*; trim the string ends.

Fig. 1

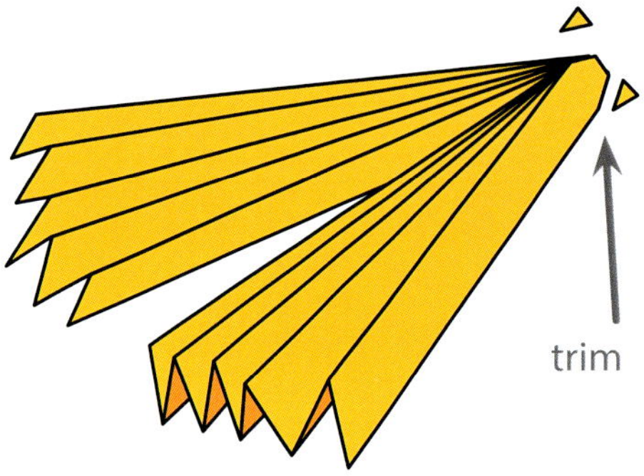

Fig. 2

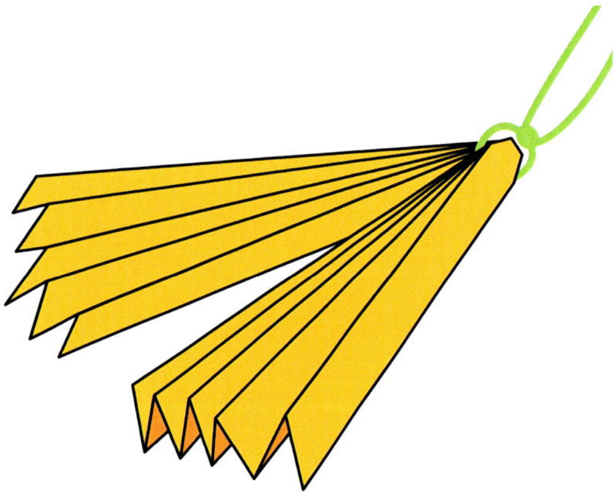

3. Trim the ends of the folded paper to a point *(Fig. 3)*.

Fig. 3

4. Pull the folds open and glue the straight edges together on each side.
5. Trim the edge of the paper circle with the decorative-edge scissors. Glue the circle to the center of the flower.
6. Punch a hole in one point. Tie a length of string through the hole to hang the flower.
7. To make smaller flowers, simply trim off more of the folded ends in Step 3.

Bottle Centerpiece

SHOPPING LIST

For each bottle:

- ☐ glass bottle
- ☐ flat white spray paint
- ☐ 8" length of green paper twine
- ☐ flower embellishment
- ☐ 8mm clear rhinestone
- ☐ flower
- ☐ hot glue gun and glue sticks

To make each Bottle:

1. Spray paint the bottle white.
2. Knot the twine around the neck of the bottle; trim the ends as desired.
3. Glue the flower embellishment to the knot. Glue the rhinestone to the center of the flower embellishment.
4. Place a flower in the bottle.

Cupcake Wrappers & Toppers

SHOPPING LIST

For each cupcake wrapper and topper:

- ☐ assorted-colored cardstock
- ☐ silver glitter cardstock
- ☐ $1^1/_2$" diameter circle paper punch
- ☐ 1"w heart-shaped paper punch
- ☐ small wood craft sticks
- ☐ hot glue gun and glue sticks
- ☐ tracing paper

To make each Cupcake Wrapper:

1. Trace the pattern, page 24, onto tracing paper; cut out. Use the pattern to cut out the cupcake wrapper from the colored cardstock.
2. Punch a heart from the glitter cardstock. Glue the heart to the center of the wrapper.
3. Wrap the paper around the cupcake and secure with glue.

To make each Topper:

1. Punch two circles from the glitter cardstock.
2. Punch two hearts from the colored cardstock.
3. Glue each heart to a circle.
4. Glue the backs of the circles together with the craft stick sandwiched in between.
5. Insert the stick in the cupcake.

Glittered Votive Holders

SHOPPING LIST

For each votive holder:

- ☐ clear glass votive holder
- ☐ votive candle
- ☐ silver glitter
- ☐ spray adhesive
- ☐ newspaper

Caution: Never leave a burning candle unattended.

To make the Votive Holder:

1. Spray the votive holder with spray adhesive.
2. Working over newspaper to catch the excess glitter, sprinkle glitter on the votive holder.
3. Place the candle in the votive holder.

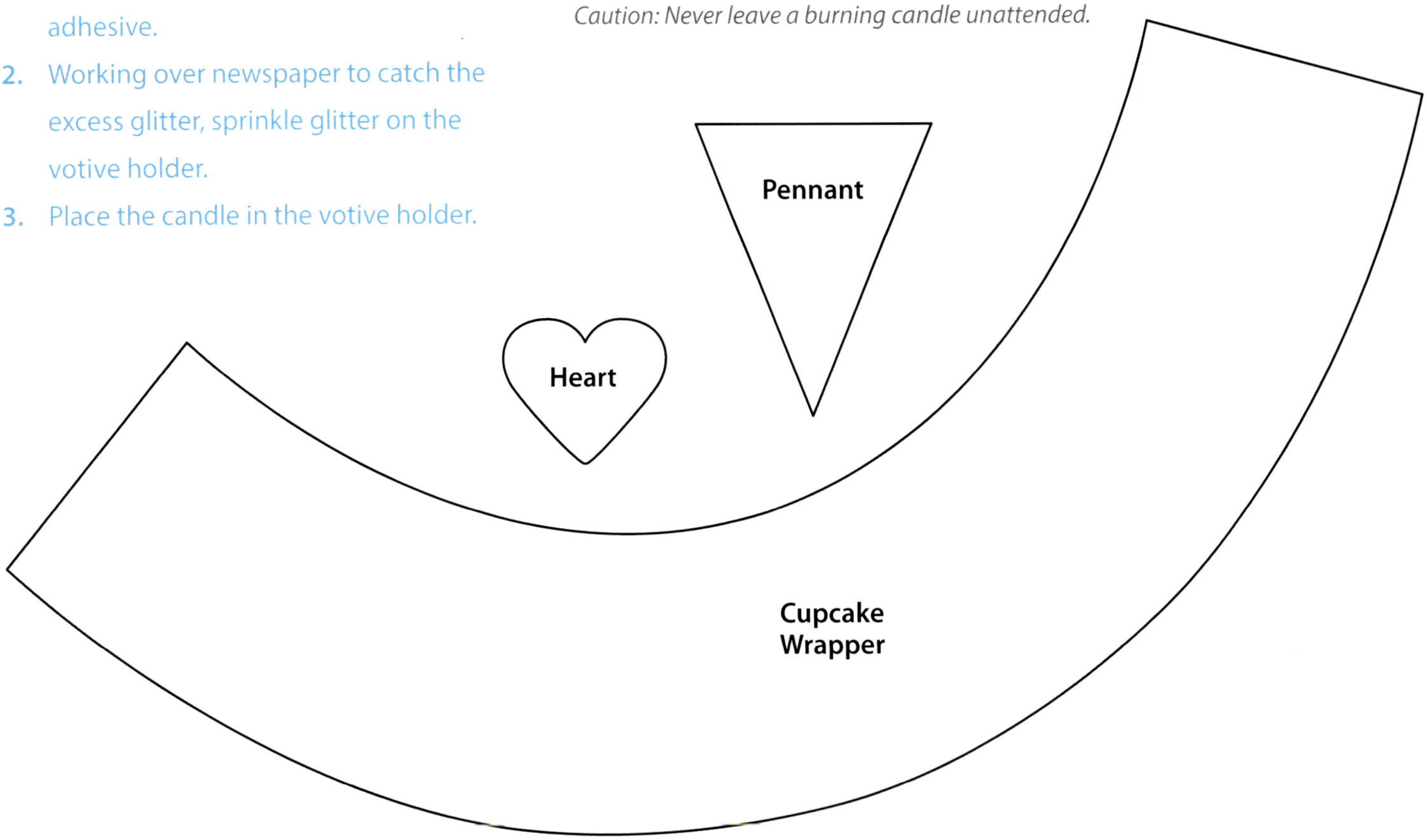

Production Team: Product Development Director: Anna L. Andrews; Designer – Kelly Reider; Contributing Designers – Kim Hamblin and Becky Werle; Technical Writer – Lisa Lancaster; Technical Associate – Mary Sullivan Hutcheson; Editorial Writer – Susan Frantz Wiles; Senior Graphic Artist – Lora Puls; Photostylist – Lori Wenger; Photographer – Jason Masters.